Cradled By The Island: Poems of Maternal Love, Chronic Illness, and Autism

Annabelle Gonzalez

BookLeaf Publishing

India | USA | UK

Presentation by *BookLeaf Publishing*

Web: www.bookleafpub.com

E-mail: info@bookleafpub.com

ISBN: 9789363305373

First edition 2024

To my children, Jaivaneese, also known as Startiism, and Jarrel: you are my inspiration, my motivation, and the very reason I strive to break cycles, become a better human, and continue to grow in all my endeavors. Every step I take is with you on my mind and in my heart, as I seek to provide you with the tools, the needles, to weave your own threads in the vast tapestry of life. Your presence in my life is a blessing, and I am grateful for the joy and purpose you bring to my existence.

XoXo

Mom

ACKNOWLEDGMENTS

To my family, who are the core of my roots and the foundation upon which I stand: your love, support, and wisdom have shaped every part of who I am. You have given me the strength to face each challenge and the courage to embrace each new chapter of my life.

To my friends, whose unwavering support has carried me through all of my new explorations: your belief in me has been a guiding light, encouraging me to push beyond my limits and embrace the unknown. Thank you for standing by my side, for celebrating my victories, and for lifting me up during difficult times.

PREFACE

In the quiet moments between day and night, when the world seems to pause and reflect, I often find myself reaching for the threads that bind my life together. These threads—woven from family, love, heritage, motherhood, resilience, and the challenges that come with autism and chronic illness—form the fabric of my existence. They are the stories I carry within me, the tales I've lived, and the lessons I've learned that I will pass on to my children.

This collection of poetry is a journey through those threads. It is an exploration of the intricate bonds of family, the rich tapestry of Puerto Rican heritage that shapes my identity, and the complexities of navigating motherhood in a world that often feels uncertain. It is a celebration of resilience, a tribute to the strength found in the face of adversity, and a testament to the beauty that emerges from even the most challenging experiences.

Writing these poems has been an act of reflection and healing. Each verse is a piece of my heart, a snapshot of the moments that have defined me and the people I hold dear. I sought to capture not just the struggles but also the joy, the laughter, and the quiet victories that come with embracing life in all its fullness.

As you turn these pages, I hope you find echoes of your own journey. Whether you are a mother, a caregiver, or someone navigating the complexities of chronic illness or the challenges of raising a child with autism, may these words offer you solace, strength, and a sense of connection. We are all woven from the threads of our experiences, and it is in sharing our stories that we find comfort and community.

Thank you for joining me on this journey. May the poems within Cradled By The Island: Poems of Maternal Love, Chronic Illness, and Autism inspire you to honor the threads that make up your own life's tapestry and find beauty and strength in the weaving!

Annabelle Gonzalez

Motherhood

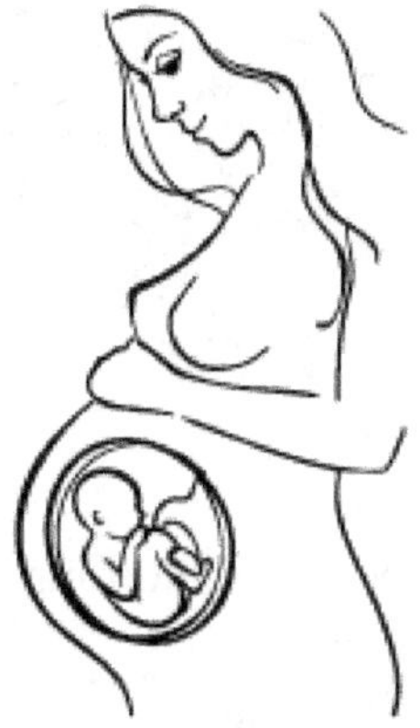

Mothers honoring tradition by
Offering lessons on culture and family
The roots that ground us and unfold
Hundreds of stories on love and life to
Entertain and guide generations
Remnants of advice and recycled recipes
Hoping to leave an impression
Of descendants who migrated
Onward to better opportunities
Doting memories renewing hope to repeat the
cycle

Roots and Wings

Sun rises
and before the beautiful morning rays
make their way up
Freshly brewed Bustelo
seeps its way through the apartment
Along with the sound
as mom pours herself a cup

Cafe con Leche is served
and I enjoy the symphony
of Pan Sobao,
I can almost
feel the warmth
and taste the butter now

I guess mom is serving up fried eggs,
perhaps a tortilla de Huevos as well
and then my senses go wild
with another tantalizing smell

Yes!!
We definitely hit the jackpot today!
I hear the clatter of the spoon
as it whips its way around the saucepan,
The melodic rhythm is like
a dotted quarter note;
one and a half beats;
in a 4/4 time signature,
such perfect measure,
Harina de Maiz,
creamy yet slightly gritty cornmeal,
a Puerto Rican treasure!

Hearty meals to start the day right,
to get out the door,
and put up a fight,
A day-to-day grind,
to represent *her*
in the best light!
Her struggles and challenges,
the poverty,
the trauma
I'm always left wondering,
how'd you keep your head up, momma

Your passions and obstacles enthrall me
to dive deep into our culture
To further understand your modus operandi,
your profound structure

To unravel the mysteries
that lie in your thoughts
and within you
To make connections...
to get a clue
To deconstruct
what others construe
To paint my mother
in the perfect hue
One that is tried,
but one that is true!

To find reason when there's no rhyme
To make sense of losing loved ones in His time
To carry the baggage that is mine
To read between the lines before I sign
To push through storms and act like I'm fine
To do things for others and expect not a dime
To fight for what's right until the end of time

Thanks to you,
I will soar through anything life brings
You have grounded my roots
and given me wings

With these wings I take flight
No matter the plight
Thank you for the threads
that have woven family bonds tight

"Mama-cum-laude"

The butcher called her "Anita la Huerfanita"

Mama, why? And she let out a little giggle
He's just fooling around; it's nothing but a riddle

With half a pound of Virginia Ham
and a pound of American Cheese
We walked to the register,
and she said, "In the book, please"

The men at the counter
politely obliged and replied,
"Your new balance is $31.25"

We left the bodega, groceries in hand
On our way to Housing Authority land

A few blocks away,
mama bumped into a friend
She stopped and chatted a bit,
so as not to offend

The lady commented,
"Out with all your kids, I see?"
"No, no, I have half a dozen;
I'm with 6, 5, 4, and this one is 3"

This one is 3! Number 3…
That would be me!

I was the oldest of the bunch
on this round
My two older sisters, Di and Diana,
were homeward bound.

Mama always refers to us as numbers
One of my greatest wonders

Nonetheless, 5 girls and 1 boy
Our mother's greatest pride and joy

Blood, sweat, and tears
Raised by a single mother
who seemingly has no fears

Grew up on food stamps and WIC
Who would imagine
all 6
would be top pick

Mama is well known
by all in town
Her child-rearing has earned her
an invisible crown

All six of us not only went to college

But
beyond knowledgeable
in our fields
Many of us leaders and experts,
thanks to our shields

Shielded by our mother's love
Shielded by the lord above

Shielded from the street
Because mama didn't skip a beat

Shielded from keeping bad company
Because mama raised us decently

Mama, the epitome of
"As strong as strong can be"

To raise 6 college graduates
in the projects alone is no small feat

Mama's limited education,
having never completed elementary school
Presented obstacles and setbacks,
but mama's no fool

Number 6 graduated
and we decided
mama deserved a cap and gown
A moment to give her
her flowers and crown

A day to acknowledge her success!

See, mama is wiser than the typical grad
Regardless, her children taught her to add

If mama's child-rearing
was equivalent to SATs,
Mama's SATs
are a perfect 16 hundred
Her entire college experience
would have been fully funded

If mama's life skills
were tallied like GPAs,
Mama's GPA

would be a perfect 4.0
She'd be on the Dean's List
and earning Summa-cum-laude
I'll have you know

No elementary school
or high school diploma
or even a GED,
But certainly,
there should be something
for such a rare breed
Until then,
She remains
our "Mama-cum-laude"

Bound by tradition

Traditions run deep in my Puerto Rican veins
From what I believe
to what I say
And what I think
and how I pray

God and Family;
the forefront of decisions that I construct
At the forefront of what I allow
and what I condone
And what I consider a house
and what I make a home

Historical influences and practices
I've adopted and some that I adjust
Including a large, close-knit family

and some gender roles
And Three Kings Day
and Quinceañeras
and how I pray for lost souls

True Red, White, and Blue
Boricua Values I'm proud to exude
The top three R's:
Religion, Respect, and Roots
Strong work ethics, education,
and community pursuits

Generosity and hospitality,
like rhumba to my Latin soul

Two powerful gifts given
to reward your loyalty to my family
To mistake my gifts
is to underestimate
karma's response uncannily

At my core is the story
of the two who created me

My father was born in 1933;
mother born in 48
Surely you see
the age difference is great

Times have changed
so their relationship
is Puerto Rican history

Bound by tradition,
where a woman
was recognized at only 15
At a Quinceañera ceremony
where a princess becomes queen

To understand,
you need to know the symbolism
behind this tradition
The dress, the court,
the Father-Daughter dance
The shoe exchange;
entering womanhood,
a cultural stance

My father was approved by the family,
deemed a good potential spouse

Bound by tradition,
he presented his case
and went on his way
Saw him once;
the introduction,
then a year later,
their wedding day

Off to Jersey to start their new life
as husband and wife
To defy social norms,
to tackle stereotypes and strife
To live the "American Dream,"
to build a respectable life

Common to marry
at a young age
for stability and to procreate
Large families, a blessing
that continues your ancestry
and adds to the legacy

We are bound by tradition;
make no discrepancy

So many questions,
we dared not to ask
even today as adults

Out of respect for privacy,
understanding adult children
remain in that place

The place where
a child may ask
but not always get

A place where
asking some questions
is seen as a threat
The place where
the answers
may lead to regret
A place where
some stories
are best to forget

My legacy is bound by tradition
Bound by the sweetest admission
I'm defined by my culture;
I'm the very definition
Of a disposition
of submission
with an acquisition
Of customs and values
of my rendition
And the recognition
that I will always be
bound by tradition!

Family and Friends

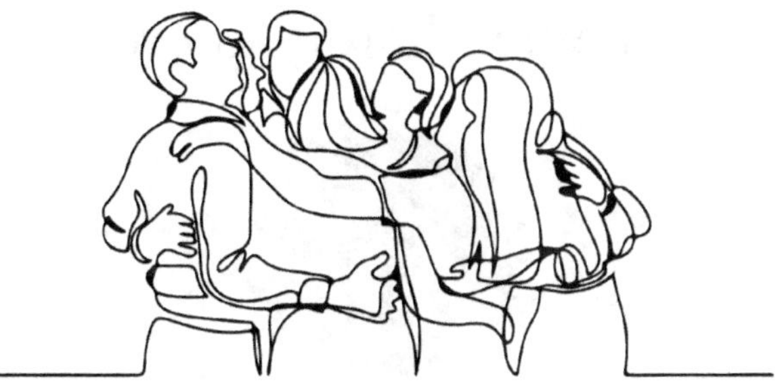

Family units are created by others
Mothers, fathers, perhaps sisters and brothers

These are the people who you see day to day
The ones who taught you to cry, laugh, and play

Friends are the family we willingly choose
The ones we connect with on similar views

Both important parts of the story of our lives
Both contributing to what makes us grow wise

Gonzalez—Shadows of a name I barely knew

Aniceto Gonzalez, also known as "Tommy,"
is somewhat of a mystery
I know many things about my father,
but not much of his history

My father was a charming
and cunning
old-school
Puerto Rican Man
An aficionado of island rhythms
Salsa, Merengue,
Boleros—a true fan

Played guitar and sang cover songs
on cassette tapes he would accrue

Hector Lavoe, Willie Colon,
Frankie Ruiz, to name a few

Loved a pastime
that would turn out
detrimental to his health
No amount of treatment could save him,
nor a plethora of wealth

Dark red, white, and blue
were the colors of choice
L & M's by the case
he'd request for any occasion
in a friendly voice

Emphysema, Hodgkin's, COPD
The perfect cocktail of toxicity

Such a shame
because otherwise,
Dad was in tip-top shape
We never anticipated a ventilator,
much less a trach

And then
a twist of fate
came banging at our door
My father's tracheotomy
wasn't an option anymore

My siblings and I
left confused and afraid
We braced ourselves
for an outcome
that inevitably
became grave

Surrounded by family,
March 26, 2009,
you took your last breath
Active and healthy,
lungs capsized;
the cause of your death

Your handiness, your humor
you had so much more life to live
But when God decides,
there's nothing you can outlive

I dare not question
He decided this was your time
But I can't lie, the pain and sequence
of your departure
followed no rhyme

We are left with memories
of the man you once were
With the stories

of when you met,
married,
and had children
with her

Memories of being driven to school
and given three dollars for lunch
Days when we could buy
two slices and a soda,
three dollars was much

Recounting the memories
of visiting your job,
observing your pride
As you pulled back the elevator gates
and wound up your ride

The place where you gained
the nickname "Tommy"
from your boss
He couldn't say your name
so he changed it;
that was a different type of loss

Stories of how you traveled
to and from Puerto Rico
The place you resided
for a time being
when mama let go

Back to your roots:
your brothers, your sisters,
your dad, and your mother
A place where
grandparents, aunts, uncles,
and cousins
all know one another

Where exactly do your roots reside?
What part of the island—
Country or Oceanside?

How many siblings did you have;
are they living
or have they crossed over
Best chance at answers
is to wish on a clover

Embedded in my very core,
the paternal last name I carry,
the roots that I sow
Now and forever
will be
Gonzalez,
shadows of a name
I barely know

"Three-Nine"

"I shine, you shine, THREE-NINE"

I can hear it as if it were being sung this very
second

It was the ever-so-popular project chant
that we dare not repeat
Mama said, "It had no place in our family;
it belonged to the street"

Three-Nine
was the name
some kids called the local gang
They had all sorts of subliminals;
some of which led kids to bang

The good old projects;
home of great sin.
Where daylight fades quickly
and dreams seldom begin

A Puerto Rican girl was I,
raised to stand strong and tall
Raised not to cower or flinch,
raised to fight
and not fall

Mama always kept us
away from the crowd
Away from anything and anyone
seemingly loud

That protective detail
worked in theory
But placed a target on our backs,
led to many a query

Why do they think
their family is above all the rest
And every once in a while,
they'd put us to the test

Playground fights,
which lead to family brawls
Which led to more participants
and police calls

The streets were tough
and the nights were long
But in our hearts,
we sang their song,

"I shine, you shine, THREE-NINE"

Roots so deep; full of grace and pride
We will not cower; we will not hide!
We will forever shine, forever "THREE-NINE!"

A Sibling Story

I take pride in announcing
I'm one of the six
4 sisters, 1 brother—
a personality mix!

Each one of us,
very different yet linked at the core
Sometimes there's peace,
and sometimes there's war!

This, of course, is common
amongst family tribes
Then, back to us
and the undeniable vibes

Those who know us
and have been in our presence
Are sure to rave
about the very essence

The essence of bonds
that are sewn tight at the roots
Our parents, our core,
taught us how to labor our fruits

Not literally,
but figuratively
through their failures and success
And we are the creation
of such a beautiful mess

Ancestral and generational traumas,
difficult to avoid
Through breaking those cycles,
the traumas destroyed

It begins with awareness
and accountability
Requires lots of work
and total involvement
for sustainability

My siblings and I are all very different,
though often compared
From the way we speak, dress, eat,
run our homes,
and style our hair

Different as we are,
regardless of what's happening from day to day
I am full of pride about family,
but most proud of my siblings, I must say

From the top to the bottom,
numbers one through six
All unique journeys,
successful futures to depict

Beyond proud of each sibling
for their individual success
Especially since, compared to others,
we had much less
But
Even with less
We thrived nonetheless!

To run down their careers
and explain it to all
I'd have to go back
before they ran, walked,
and crawled

So here's a snapshot
of how they have grown
From thriving careers
to owning a home

A nurse who worked long,
difficult shifts
Now a nursing administrator,
overseer of conflicts

A wonder with numbers
and a lover of math
Takes on the business world;
the Technology Buyer Path

A brainiac for sure;
graduate of U M D N J
Testing samples, diagnostic reports,
answers underway

A justice seeker,
definitely a speaker!
Carrying out civil duties
Utilizing legal enforcements
with some reinforcements

Lastly,
A lover of performing arts;
Influencing future musicians;
touching their hearts
A uniquely beautiful voice,
Yet behind-the-scenes
teaching was her choice!

A wonderfully talented and intelligent crew...
As a result of dreams,
they decided to pursue

My Tribe, My Village

Where do I begin to describe
The beautiful women
who make up my tribe

To name them all
would not pay enough homage
The heart, the loyalty,
the love, and the unending knowledge

Instead, I believe
describing them would be best
Be prepared to be a bit envious
and definitely impressed

These women are women
who age like fine wine
A perfect blend of sassy and hood
yet elegant and divine

My tribe rolls deep,
friendships run decades old
Let's start with the fierce diva,
the Greek goddess mold

Practically grew up together;
yes, we're close in age
Patience and kindness,
candles, church, and sage

Your husband, a dear friend;
your kids simply rock
I value your advice and guidance
about tending to my flock

Next is J's teacher
who entered my life
When not only J,
but my love life
was pure strife

Represents love for others
regardless of DNA
A big heart and always
something positive to say
She will warm up your heart
and lighten up your day

Can't forget my girl
the one not to mess with
The nails, the lashes,
the Yankee cap, the Bronx fit

A tower of strength
amidst adversity
Representing paternity, maternity,
fraternity, and diversity

The one who does it all
doesn't cower or fall,
The one who drops everything
to answer my call

My life wouldn't be complete
without girls from my past
The ones who helped me
paint the town and have a blast

My freckled Scottish connoisseur of N Y C
The one who showed me how to live carefree
Does Falucka, Latin Quarters, Drama, and Nells
Le Bar Bat, Tropicana, and Copa ring bells?

Let's not forget my Caribbean queen,
a jack of all trades
From a blue-collar worker
to getting the grades

An aide, social worker,
broker, to mention a few
But the most impressive
is the quest that is new
The one that began
with her love of food!

"Double back and taste it,"
a true delight!
Realtor by day,
Food Truck owner by night!

And where would I be
without my petite and feisty
Italian gal
The one I call upon
for questions on morale

A boy mom
and teacher,
Great advice,
my own preacher

Her smile doesn't falter or fail,
attentive to every detail
No situation will ever destroy her;
she will not derail

She's the voice of reason
when I am without
The one I can depend on,
never a doubt

Top-tier advice
on motherhood
and relationships
As if she has memorized
life's scripts!

Last but not least,
one is new to my crew
Started as my colleague
and now a friend who is true

Honest and Fair, CONFIDENT!
Smooth like butter
A mother, a sister,
a cousin like no other

A heart twice the size
what her cavity holds
She reminds me daily
of the values I uphold

In this place called life
where our success is ours alone
It's our support systems,

our villages…
that help set the tone

For those who surround you,
your village, your tribe
Are what the doctor
prescribed to survive!

Relationships

Relationships are an inevitable part of life
Everyone plays a role
Lessons or blessings
And eventually, the beauty subsides
Till the day one decides
It isn't worth the bumpy ride
Onto the next adventure, a new lesson learned
New experiences, old scars
Sadness and pain
Having to put yourself out there again
If only a real one would step in and reign
Push forward with your head held high
Set an example for your kids; you will get by

Nevermore

I am a hopeless romantic
and it shouldn't be a surprise
From things that are planned and perfect
to things that you improvise

If this is the case,
can someone explain why
I've never been married,
haven't given it a try

Well... sit back and relax,
and enjoy the show
I'm about to embark
on a journey
you didn't quite know
With a little help from my favorite poet,
Mr. Edgar Allen Poe

See, once upon a college query,
I met a young man
I thought was endearing

I basically found myself
weak and weary,
I wish someone had said,
"Snap out of it, deary!"

But the pitter-patter of my heart
wouldn't skip a beat
Getting him out of my head
was a battleless feat

Needless to say,
we became joined at the hip
I knew I was in
for a special trip

I wish someone would've told me
this trip was full of haze
It could have saved me
some of the most painful days

Returned the ring,
My relationship is over... NEVERMORE...
Like Poe's "The Raven"
Reality came tap, tap, tapping on my door

This relationship is over! NEVERMORE!

Took some time to heal
and set out once more
Another adventure,
I stepped into love's open door

This one was better,
most definitely, than the last
With him, I had
such a beautiful blast

Showered with affection,
gifts, and more
Put me on a pedestal so high,
'til it crashed to the floor

Returned the ring,
My relationship is over... NEVERMORE...
Like Poe's "The Raven"
Reality came tap, tap, tapping on my door
This relationship too is over! NEVERMORE!

By now this hopeless romantic
was just sick
Heart stone cold,
solid as a brick!

I'm never doing that!

Not ever in my life!
I will never become someone's
sad, quiet wife!

The dreams and visions I had
Went from good to bad

I have no more left in me to give,
Let me move on; I have a life to live

There was some living,
and the living was real!
Now, I have a baby
and this living is a big deal

For her, I turn over a brand new leaf
I will not surrender my heart to a thief

My relationship is over... NEVERMORE...
Like Poe's "The Raven"
Reality came tap, tap, tapping on my door
This relationship is over! NEVERMORE!

And then I remember,
a Chilly December
I met someone not quite my type
and a friendship began
I wish I hadn't entertained it,
but I did and I ran

This one was different,
accepted a package deal
To simultaneously love two humans at once,
seemed very surreal

I wish they had told me
to run for the hills
From this one's dark and deceptive skills

Returned the ring,
My relationship is over... NEVERMORE...
Like Poe's "The Raven"
Reality came tap, tap, tapping on my door
This relationship is over! NEVERMORE!

Lots of reflecting,
giving me grace, love, and light
Couldn't do marriage,
if not done right!

So much more to it
than saying yes to the dress
If not done right,
it becomes a big, sloppy mess

I value the idea...
to have and to hold
Because

I want it forever
until we are old

I honor the strength behind
sickness and health
Alongside your partner
in poverty and wealth

I welcome the challenges,
the good times, and the bad,
But I appropriately grieve
the loss of a love I never had

Silent Treatment

Abuse is a shapeshifter
Like an unexpected drifter
Until It finds its place
And you come face to face

Abuse can come in many forms
More often than not,
it transforms
Sometimes it's physical
and sometimes it's mental
Regardless of which one,
they're both detrimental

A type of abuse
that is often not discussed
Is one that evokes
feelings of disgust and mistrust

The one where no doors are slammed
The one that is most hard to understand
It's the one where silence is the weapon in hand

A thousand things
you'll never say
And yet it hurts
in every way
Your eyes don't meet;
your lips won't part
You shut me out,
a skillful art

Not shouting or enraged
Just simply disengaged

Words left unsaid
are undermined
They still leave scars
inside my mind

To withhold communication
Without any explanation
Creates an uncomfortable situation

And further separation
Due to the isolation
And the speculation
Of complication and desperation
A huge violation
And contamination
Of our relation
Without mediation

You build walls of silence around me
Empty air, a vacant stare
As if I'm not even there
And you're not even aware
How very unfair
To receive your glare
Avoidant of care
So I have to declare
That after some prayer
This tear
Is beyond repair

Each breath I take
feels out of place
Just a lonely echo
in this loveless space.

"Annie BaeBee"

I'm not typically the type
To fall for the lines
To get drawn in by the hype

I guess the powers that be
Decided to play a cruel little trick on me

At first sight,
your presence was truly unique
I looked at your eyes
and they looked right through me
They were so endearing,
thought I heard your soul speak
Then immediately
I began to feel weak

I had no idea what you were about
until your words graced my ears
Surrounded by a sea of your peers
and some other profiteers
Line by line,
you captivated me,
but your mouth racketeers
Because it appears
That you have some fears,
Pent-up trauma from years,
A failed marriage and career,
Toxicity rears its ugly head and interferes
And any chance of you and I disappears
Left with your memories,
such stupid souvenirs!

Something about
the way you called me "Annie Baebee"
Put my mind at rest;
it set my soul free

You were supposed to be different from the rest
The one NO ONE could compare to,
My absolute BEST!

You brought the sunshine in
when there was nothing but clouds
But then you became
the thunder and rain

Inflicted your pain
Had me feeling insane
And second guessing
Such disdain

Left me puzzled and clueless
Left me hanging... Ruthless!

A cold morning message,
with some sort of apology
Containing a plethora
of reverse psychology
With your rambling choice of terminology
And through the methodology
Of your technology
You explained your toxicology
And your ideology
With some nonsense about astrology
Instead of sticking to anthropology
You continued with your mythology
Of the toxicology
It was plain criminology!

Not angry, but confused
To be led on and amused
Leaves me unenthused
And lowkey feeling used

Someone to practice all of your lines
Some motivation for your rhymes
None of your motives align
I wonder if you realize it undermines
The new person you so define
As you walk into the present time

I wish you luck, I wish you well
I wish I never completely fell
Under your seductive spell
No longer "Annie BaeBee,"
Just simply . . .
Annabelle

Autism Journey

From one day to the next, your life can change
It's a feeling that's foreign, a feeling so strange

To have no control over turning back time
No way to get back the days, life was a rhyme

Feelings of helplessness, both day and night
Dealing with darkness in pursuit of the light

Unpredictable outcomes, so much to explore
Wanting to learn and do so much more

Accepting reality makes the journey take flight
Be mindful and pray not to lose sight
You need to be strong to put up a fight!

Looking Forward to Rainbows

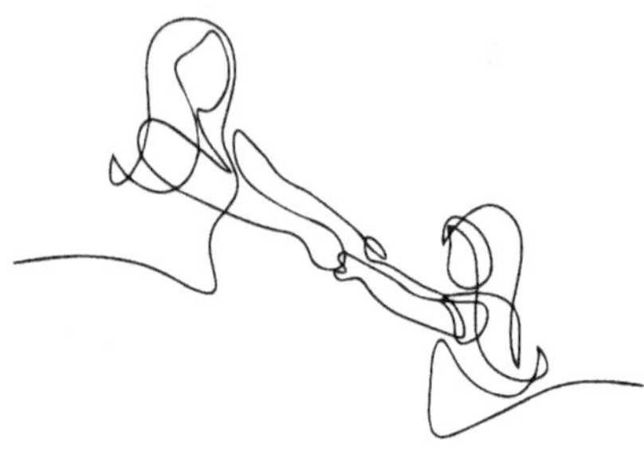

Diagnosed with Autism
before the age of two
My precious little baby
lost everything she once knew

A child who began
walking at 10 months and talking galore
Would lose her language, lose eye contact,
was aggressive, and much more

A long road ahead, the professionals would say
There's a chance she won't speak again,
but a chance that she may

Began services at home
from sun up to sun down
Therapists had her exploring
everything in town

"Tacting" was a type of intervention
she would receive
Hand over hand
and a long list of goals to achieve

Receiving two hours a day
of developmental intervention
I needed to do something
to ensure her comprehension

Made it my mission to emulate
what she received at our home
Focused on giving her a fighting chance,
she was not in this fight alone

I began with flashcards containing
an image and a word
Who would have known the magnitude,
the significance of the picture of a bird

One day while out tacting
with her therapist, Celina
We stepped out into a new World,
a usual arena

There was something in the way
she was one with the World
She dropped and she stimmed
and she ran and she twirled

There was a meltdown at the park
and we decided that was it
Two adults defeated
by a toddler's fit

As we approached our block
with Jaiva in hand, a bird flew by
She stopped and she looked right up to the sky

Joint attention was a goal on her IFSP
Who would have thought
she'd master this goal
right in front of me

But that wasn't all we would witness that day
She pointed to the sky
and her first word she would say

"Bird! Bird!" It was cheerful and clear!
Celina and I looked at each other
and began to cheer!

At that point, I thanked the Lord up above
For giving us strength,
for gracing us with His love

For carrying me
when my spirits were down

For instilling some hope
when I was overcome with doubt

Her Autism Journey has been filled
with many ups and downs
With thunder and rain,
with happiness and frowns

With tiny moments of victories
that open new doors
Like when the rain subsides
and the sun wins the war

It gifts us with rainbows
for a very short window
It keeps us enthralled
and in a state of limbo

Wondering if we'd ever
catch it again
Like when she said bird,
and I shouted AMEN!

How I look forward
to the rainbows in her life
Small but significant victories
that come after experiencing strife

City Lights, Quiet Fights

Our relationship was over
before we moved back to my hometown city
Over before I was pregnant,
we tried just for her, what a pity

Regardless,
we talked about giving it a good last try
At least one of us did
until you called with a dry goodbye

I wasn't surprised because we were headed in
that direction
But the way you went about it,
the way you left,
was a puzzling insurrection

The unforgettable day you called me to say.
"Just want to let you know,
I won't be coming home today"

I thought it was a joke for goodness sake,
"I heard what you said
Are you pulling my leg;
has your brain just gone dead?!"

No particular fight or incident had occurred,
Just you doing you and exiting absurd

All your belongings gone,
I was oblivious to this
How did I not notice,
drawers and closet empty,
What did I miss?!

Looking back I now know
what was obvious to all
I was going through a lot,
fighting another internal brawl

Trying to keep myself together
amidst my father's untimely death
Fighting images, sounds, and smells
of the hospital, where he took his last breath

Adapting to losing a parent
and moving to a new apartment
Registering her for school,
reading the IEP's fine print

I was working days
you had begun working nights
Barely passed each other at home,
hence no fights

I dealt with the night-time routines and her rage
You got her ready for school,
turning a new page

You left when she was at her worst
and didn't look back
That was a cowardly
and sneaky
dirty attack

Hung up the phone
and needed a few minutes to process
Mom was the first call;
Needed someone to watch her,
What a mess!

City lights and quiet fights
were the theme of my new story
As I picked myself up,
figured things out,
her tantrums in full glory

The new normal was trying,
but I had to push through
So many daily little things to get done
had to be done askew

From taking out the trash
to washing all our clothes
To digging out my snowed-in car
and showering, some of my new woes

Remembered the difficulty
tying her to a harness around my waist
While I brought down our garbage bags,
she looked so displaced

Had to ensure she wouldn't take flight,
She'd elope and drop with all of her might

Mornings on Saturdays began
at 5 a.m. on the dot
Be the first at the washers,
my weekly thought

Flashbacks of praying
that she remains safe and asleep
Ran down 3 flights of stairs,
a new laundry marathon sweep

The fear of her waking up and walking outside,
The fear of her trapping herself alone INSIDE!

So many fears and things to consider
Why did you leave this way,
started feeling bitter

But thanks to my mother's strength
and the Lord above
They reminded me of the strength
of a mother's love

For in the midst of City Lights and Quiet Fights,
A mother's love
will make you soar to new heights!

Why My Caged Bird Sings

If Ms. Angelou were here today,
I wouldn't hesitate to share
Her poetry inspires me to dig deep;
inspires me to go bare

Reading her words,
I focus on what speaks to me
"Caged Bird" is a picture
of my daughter's biography

You see, the FREE BIRD represents
the neurotypical
Who makes leaps and bounds;
it measures a pinnacle

It commands the great sky
While others are passed by
No matter how hard you try
Almost impossible to fly high

The other, CAGED BIRD, is neurodiverse
Navigating life in this cryptic metaverse

She sits in her cage
and stares at the sky
Contained by her cage
as the world waves goodbye

How this beautiful creature desires to be free
But as much as she tries, this reality can not be

She spreads her colorful wings and gives it a try
Then plops to the base,
"How I wish to fly high!"

She picks herself up and back on her rod
Perhaps if I sing, I'll summon a squad

My caged bird opens her mouth
and begins doing her thing
A powerful belted message
this caged bird would sing

A message of hope and a future so bright
For a quick sullen second, she loses all sight

Lost sight of the bars
that obstruct her view
A vision so strong,
easy for most birds to construe

Visions of dreams interrupted
by nightmarish screams
Of a daunting reality
of incessant routines

Caged bird,
you're not meant to remain here forever
You are by far
too talented,
too sweet,
and too clever

Heighten your senses
and be keen with your sight
For when there's an opening,
think quick and take flight

The cage is where you landed,
not where you came to be
So go look for the opening
because you hold the key

There's so much out there
the world has yet to be seen
From a lyrical caged bird
who's only 18!

Rainbows in My Life: Through Her Eyes

I hate it when people say,
"Life isn't all rainbows."
As if I don't get
life isn't exactly great all the time
As if I believe
what's mine is yours
and what's yours is mine

As if going to school
and getting good grades
make everything fine
As if I don't struggle
day to day to get up,
to rise and shine

My life hasn't been all rainbows,
but I'll tell you one thing,
regardless,
I always look for those

My life has been filled
With hardships and pain
With thunder and rain
With feeling insane

See, while I may have been too little to tell
Into a deep, dark silence I quickly fell

Lost my language after my 1st birthday
A drastic change,
those around me would say

Rain…

No language, no eye contact,
no way to say, "I'm not feeling well"
or to say I have pain

Rain…

Massive outbursts, aggression,
and therapists galore
So much life stuff
to learn and explore

Suffering and distress
Little girl, your life is a mess!

All my young life
I was basically in rehabilitation
Early intervention, my treatment,
was no vacation
Onlookers judging me...
total humiliation

Rain…

On one warm and typical day
As I ran up and down with my corky sway

I looked up and spotted a bird

BIRD!

BIRD!

Bird was my first word!
I got my voice back!

Rain…

As the clouds began to subside,
Parts of me were coming alive!

Peering through the clouds
after the rain passed was the sun!

There's so much fun
To be had in the sun

But wait

What's this?

A rainbow!

A beautiful rainbow!

It's what my life is.

There's thunder and rain,
Sadness and pain
Moments that are insane

But then

The sun emerges and the beautiful combination
Eliminates all the frustration

Even if for a few moments,
minutes, even a second...
A new me is sure to beckon

Life is not all rainbows, but I can say 100%
I totally look forward
to many rainbows in my life

Unfairness and Choice: Jaiva's Journey

There's a thought that always puzzles me
When you look at me, what exactly do you see?

Well, I'm sure you can't miss
the bouncy brown curls
But, honestly,
Do I look like other teen girls?

I mean, I can appear bubbly and friendly,
Not to mention I think I can be quite trendy,

I suppose, I'm much like your typical teen,
But something more remains unseen

There's a thought that always puzzles me
When you look at me,
Do you see invisible disability?

Only invisible because of your perception
I'm somewhat of an anomaly,
some misconception

Only a disability because
of stupid milestone expectations
Developmental delays
causing catastrophic tribulations

Unfairness and Choices

I stand before you today
To share my truth;
I have much to say

I am no longer the child
Who acted all wild

The one who threw a fit
The one who bit and spit

The one who lined toys up in rows
The one who reacted with powerful blows

I bet you think that I have it good,
That things are turning out the way they should,

I've had to make choices that weren't too easy
and weren't quite right
including a decision,
I make public tonight.

A few days before I was to dawn
my cap and gown
Instead of feeling joy and happiness,
I began feeling down

With tears in my eyes and a fast-beating heart
I uttered the words, my adult life cannot start.

I need more support
and I've much yet to learn
courtesy of a failed system,
like clearance at a store
Final Sale! No return!

Thanks to my mother,
I learned I have a right
to take control of my schooling,
I can put up a fight

Unfairness and Choices

There's a thought that always puzzles me...
When I look at me, what exactly do I see?

I see a not-so-typical, typical teen girl
Who yearns to learn and take on the world

Who isn't afraid to stand up and yell
I am who I am!
And those who don't care for me
Can go to hell!

I am Jaivaneese Johnson, aka Startiism
A not-so-typical, typical teen girl

Who was gifted a powerful voice
Who has dealt with unfairness,
but recently made a choice

And today I say it with pride for all to hear,
I've opted for a second senior year!

A second senior year!
Not retained or held back
Time to get my life on the right track

A chance to take back
what I am owed
A chance to reap
from the benefits that I will sow

Due to limited language
and extreme behaviors

I spent my entire life in special schools
Learning non-traditionally
with a variety of tools

While others learned their ABCs and 123s
I spent my days crying
and dropping to my knees

While others learned
addition and subtraction
how to multiply, divide,
and convert a fraction

I was working on one or two-step commands,
how to keep my body still,
how to not stim with my hands.

Unfairness and Choices

Two years ago, I announced
I wanted to go to college
But how could I do so
with such limited knowledge

I transitioned into the world of regular education
Part time in one world
and part time in another
Two days at one school
and 3 days at the other

I quickly realized how much I had truly missed
Overflow me with academics!
I must succeed,
I insist!

As hard as I worked to get a GPA of 3.88
I felt I could do better;
such pressure, such weight!

I applied and got accepted
into FDU and Ramapo,
Only to decide
I wasn't ready to go.

Unfairness and Choices

There's a thought that always puzzles me
When I look at me, what exactly do I see?

2025, I choose me!
On my terms, at my pace
There is no rush!
My life is not a race.

College life and career
are not pending, just deferred
As a result of
what a not-so-typical, typical girl preferred!

Religion

Religion is my foundation
Elevating hope
Leading to peace
Insecurities cease and this I preach
God, the Father, determines my path
I wouldn't be here if not for His grace
Only person I can talk to at any location
No judgment or worries; with Him I am safe

After Confirmation

Raised by a hard-core Catholic,
we attended mass weekly
Mother walked around town with conviction,
but about church meekly

Had us attend CCD
to complete all our sacraments
Sacraments
A part of our legacy imprints

Beginning with Baptism,
ending with Holy Orders or Matrimony
All of them accompanied
by some meaningful ceremony

Fast Forward—today, and where am I now?
I'm teaching Confirmation in my hometown

Confirmation, a sacrament of initiation,
one done by choice
A decision to portray the Catholic way...
In your own voice!

This is typically done
when you are in high school
Toughest of times;
teens don't view this as cool

Attend class and mass
because the family pressure is great
It's not typically God that leads them
to follow their faith

Fears of what happens
after they commit
Fears of failing to live
the way He sees fit

The future is unknown
and some can't see why
The only choices are to serve Him
or to marry before you die

But if we're in love with them,
why do I have to get married,
What if I want a life that's more varied?

Why isn't there room
to try an alternate lifestyle?
As long as the living
is gentle, not hostile

As a teacher,
I answer the questions and say
If Confirmation is what you want,
then we live the Catholic way

There's a reason for the teachings and guidance
We can live happy and fruitful lives
When we choose compliance

It's difficult to fully understand what that means
Because you are young
and have ideas busting at the seams

The truth of the matter is
we all have our own relationship with God
But be very mindful and careful,
the living is not a facade

The Lord loves and accepts
sinners and saints all the same
Especially when working
to improve decisions in His name

There's no perfect being
except the Lord above
Who will cradle and shower you
with protection and love

He does not wish
to see His children in pain
This is why
we do not take life or his teachings in vain

We try our best to serve Him
and others in the things we say and do
Coming to that realization...
that's when you'll know exactly what's for you!

Confirmation is an opening to His door
After confirmation, you use life to explore

The many rooms inside His house

Some filled with questions
Some filled with doubts

Some, where you feel welcomed
Some, where you're left out

Some you wished you never stepped foot in
Some you will never want to leave

But the truth of the matter is
after Confirmation
You take all of the information
That's been given to you
from creation
About the Lord
for some inspiration
With the help
of your congregation
Who will provide you
with validation
About your inclination
That your interpretation
and association
With God, the most high
is a representation
Of the communication
of your identification
With your religion…

And the determination
To see peace in Him
and
regulation
And
honor Him
with
Cooperation

Irony and Illness

Illness invades your body; a total invasion
Only moments of peace on some occasion

The devastating effects of living unwell
Can leave you feeling like an empty shell

With support and love, you put up a fight
The tougher it gets, the stronger your might

Illnesses bring about an irony
many can't comprehend
What's meant to break you
gets a fight 'til the end

Forever Linked; Her Protector, His Joy

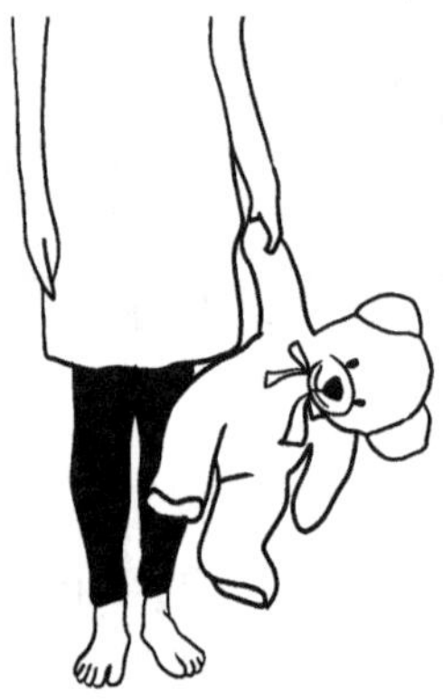

Having dealt with the reality
of my daughter's diagnosis
I began considering
her developmental prognosis

Although we worked
intensely with professionals
Her aggression increased
by about a thousand decibels

It was difficult for her
to communicate what she had to say
Seemed impossible for us
to figure out a way

Successes were there, but they were far and few
Utilized traditional methods
and some that were new

Though she learned some signs
and a few single words
She had mastered some nouns,
but couldn't understand verbs

She'd drop and she'd throw things;
she'd scream, cry, and bite
Every passing hour, every single day,
a new daunting fight

Thoughts of the future flooded my head
Took over my sleep; I lay restless in bed

As much as it terrifies me to admit
A decision burned inside me
and the flame remained lit

I asked flat out,
"Consider having another child?"
He paused for a few seconds,
looked at me, and smiled

Couldn't help but ask
a follow-up question too...
"There's a chance they'd be autistic too;

Is that okay with you?"

The reply was something
I never expected to hear
"Whether they are or they aren't,
we're armed with gear
I have one, you have one,
we're experts; nothing to fear"

With that response, we took a chance
and created her forever link
We would work tirelessly and endlessly
to keep them in sync

So many things to consider
and so much joy to be had
Welcoming a new baby
and honoring my dad

This time was different
in so many ways
We worked with her therapist
for days upon days

We shared our fears
and she responded without doubt
"I'm excited for you all,
don't worry about Jaiva,
we'll figure it out"

Didn't babyproof our house
the way most families would
We consulted with her,
ensuring Jaiva's needs were understood

At the end of all the talking,
she chuckled and said
"We need to Jaiva-proof the baby instead"

Just like that, we were off to Babies R Us
during a session
Jaiva oblivious;
Jenna laughing
at my scared expression

We started with the furniture,
the most important on her list
Tested out cribs
to find the one most of her weight would resist

She'd have her step on the edge
and have her lean in
Some of them rocked, tipped, and wobbled,
but one was a win!

That crib was solid
as solid can be
Wouldn't even tip

with a 6-month pregnant me!

Jarrel Ancieto
was born in February of 2013
The most precious sight
Jaiva had seen

She looked at him
at first with puzzled eyes
Then leaned over
and kissed him to our surprise!

Her protector, his joy
You are beyond special, little boy

Forever Linked,
brother and sister side by side
To endure and enjoy
life's roller coaster ride

No turn is too steep
for two people bound by a mother's love
Together you can do anything;
grandpa's watching from above

Lupus Journey

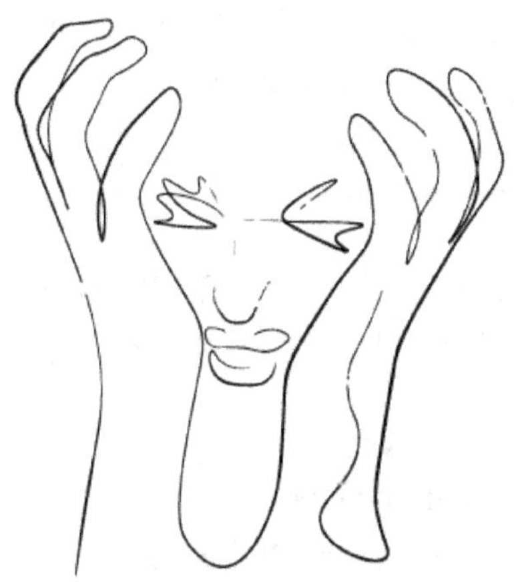

Days began with overwhelming pain
Stiffness and dizziness I couldn't explain

Perhaps it's arthritis;
a few pills will get me through
But even the strongest of pills
over the counter
wouldn't do

Eyelids so heavy; I can't explain why
Exhausted by day, by night; can't sleep if I try

As days go by, I need time to move
To get out of bed and get in the groove

Takes me about an hour
to put some pep in my step
Discovering now…
morning routines need more prep
Going to the doctor
must be the next step

Perhaps it's the age that is finally catching up
But why does it hurt to lift a small cup

Blood work was taken,
received a call the next day
Referring you to Rheumatology
and sent me on my way
Your levels are back;
you have a positive ANA

These results indicate
that something's not quite right
But a specialist can review,
further test, and give insight

And so my journey began
With a laundry list of tests they ran

Diagnosed with Lupus
and I went on with my day
Prescribed a regiment of medication;
"You should be okay"

Medication should kick in
about two months after that
The pain medication;
well, that is more stat

What wonderful news
to take on vacation
We were all set
and paid for our annual staycation
We travel to North Carolina
to spend a week with family
To tan and to swim;
to end summer happily

Can't imagine
things could get much worse,
Lucky for me, I was on vacation
with my sister, the nurse

Her friend and coworker were there as well
Into a deep zombie state, I quickly fell

I spent days and nights
just laying in bed
Slept for hours and hours;
baby months old,
couldn't be fed

I couldn't hold him,
play with him,
put him to sleep
No engagement,
entertainment,
didn't socialize; not a peep

My third day in bed,
The nurses finally said

Off to the pool you go;
you have no choice!
Moving your muscles in the water
will help you rejoice

Needed help getting dressed
and getting outside
Never expected a vacation like this;
total downside

The energy it took
to move one arm and the other
My kids looking at me;
their sick and helpless mother

That was by far
the worst trip I ever did make
I missed out on everything,
for goodness sake!

The worst was the guilt
that destroyed me inside
I wanted to run,
disappear, and hide

What is this beast invading my soul?!
Violating my body and taking its toll

Every waking hour,
a daily new fight
Until the Plaquenil
begins to take flight

The nausea, the dizziness
my system is weak
Ordinary peaceful days
are all that I seek

All these symptoms I'm having,
I'm in despair
Only became worse
when I started losing my hair

Bimonthly visits to the specialist;
assess my titers
I realized in the waiting room,
We are ALL fighters!
This beast will not defeat me;

no merit in my life will it hold
For I have a life to live
that is fruitful and bold

I have two beautiful children
who need a functioning mother
I must take care of them
and they will care for each other

This journey I'm on;
I'm not alone
And I will continue to fight
until my children are grown
and on their own!

Small Frame, Mighty Power

I cannot express
how important it is
To not overlook
a single thing
shared by your kids

No matter how big,
no matter how small
It only takes
but one simple call

A call that can put
your mind at ease
Call the doctor, provider,
therapist, or teacher, please

He was only 9
when the first sign came to light
While washing the dishes,
I heard a shout
a voice echoed of fright

Rushed to the bathroom
as fast as I could
To discover
blood on a wipe
this can't be good!

Asked the common questions
moms may
Did you hurt yourself,
push too hard,
engage in odd play?

Tried to remain calm
so he wouldn't freak out
It's ok, things happen;
if it happens again,
give me a shout

As I walked away,
wondering what could this be?
He's been constipated before
but never did bleed

Perhaps some rare occurrence;
we'll just have to wait
To see if he bleeds again
on a later date

The very next day
it happened again
He screamed from the bathroom;
I knew it then

Something's not right,
but was I in for a surprise
Wasn't simply on the wipe;
I couldn't believe my eyes

The bowl, a sea of blood
and he asked shakily
"Mom, Mom
what's happening to me?"

I tried to remain calm,
but I heard my voice crack
I'm calling the doctor;
he'll call me right back

We had an appointment
first thing, very next day
They're reasons for bleeding;
we'll order tests right away

The results came back
within 24 hours
That was the beginning
of the downpour of showers

He tested positive for Crohn's and colitis,
but it's no diagnosis
I'm referring you to pediatric GI
for treatment and prognosis

We visited his GI,
whom he'd seen before
To undergo tests,
provide information and more

He had a series of scans
and his first endoscopy stat
The biopsies returned
and we had a long chat

Stomach was in terrible shape,
chronic inflammation
Surprised he wasn't in more pain,
provided information

Began some steroids
for his stomach to heal
Just the beginning
of a lifelong ordeal

They couldn't yet diagnose him;
it was not enough to tell
Told to monitor;

if symptoms became worse, call her cell

The new normal was daily bleeding
and it didn't stop there
He began having attacks
of intestinal pain, he couldn't bear

The attacks would last about an hour;
he was unable to walk
Several emergency room visits
and then another GI talk

His symptoms don't match;
this doesn't make sense
Results of the endoscopy showed no signs
of something so intense

More meds to stop the spasms
and ease his pain
Several absences from school,
a child who was drained

Suspected mild Crohn's,
but need the labs to support
It would be difficult to justify
biologics of that sort

The difficulty stems from a child so young
on this type of disparity

He'd be receiving
a special type of chemotherapy

So in less than a year,
he went under again
and yet again
Three times a charm
when we met with the doctor then

Results of the capsule camera were in,
what was thought to be mild...
Was active and chronic
and running wild

We had our diagnosis
and treatment plan within that week
His lifelong battle
with a condition at its peak

Every 4 weeks,
an adventure with every admission
Until he gets to 8 weeks,
what's considered remission!

This year has been full
of trials and tribulations
And conversations with stipulations
Of observations and regulations
With situations and explanations

And many considerations
That brought on frustrations

But

His small frame has mighty power
He fights Crohn's at every hour

He has no battle scars for the world to see
His condition is master of invisibility

So we fight other battles
in the community and at school
To battle ignorance,
address comments,
and alter some rules

He has a right to live a full life with dignity
Free of judgment, obstacles, and malignity!

Obstacles and Journeys

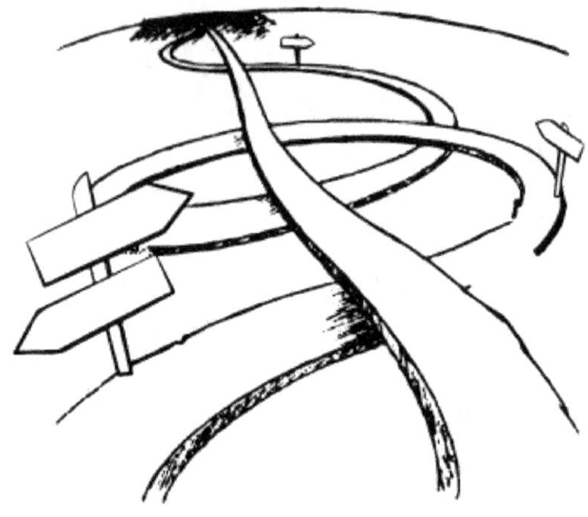

Jarringly, life can take a turn
Obstacles can lead to journeys
Ups and downs, hope, and helplessness
Realizing there are things you cannot control
Needless to say, you live and you learn
Every door that closes brings one that opens
You through the obstacles;
Stand tall and proud and carry on

A Mother's Struggle

"Once you have kids, Your life is over,"
Mama would say
I always thought this was ridiculous,
and yet here we are today

Her statement, she didn't mean literally,
She meant in the sense of living liberally

See, when you become a mother,
everything changes
You learn about sacrifice
when you have to divide your wages

You can't always just pick up and leave
Having a social life is deemed a reprieve

Your career choice and path are often affected
Can't always do exactly what you expected

So you alter your studies,
promotions deferred
Because the lines between mom and boss
are now blurred
Because employers require
their females undeterred
This ideal, totally absurd
Simply because society preferred
Not to promote someone with a herd

No matter the knowledge a mother holds inside
Her first priority and gut instinct is to provide
To lead and to guide
And yet mother's put aside
Their rightful pride
In the skills they predefined
In courses they applied
To which they tried
To share the knowledge supplied
Knowledge to which others heavily relied
Only for the powers that be to decide
Being a mother and a leader doesn't coincide
Even when the mother complied

To abide and apprise
Directives to guide in stride
Overlooked and chastised
Mother's are inclined
To realign
Because they are confined
To prioritize a design
Of a gift so divine
Our children, our spine
Until the end of our time!

"The Thread that Binds Us"

In this big, beautiful world
where we have limited time and space
It's important to recognize
people who make up your solid base
The ones who hold a special place
Filled with wonderful stories
and magical dates

In this big, beautiful world
where we have limited time and space
It's important
to live your life and fully embrace
All of your experiences,
whatever the case
And document these moments
so we leave behind a trace

In this big, beautiful world
where so much can be lost in translation
It's important to provide
the information
To our future generation
A message of salvation
and dedication
Through affirmations
that provide motivation
And inspiration
With the utmost dedication
A beautiful combination
Of an explanation
Of our salvation
Without misinterpretation

In this big, beautiful world
where the thread that binds us
Is one that defines us
And one that refines us

I want to leave behind
A piece of my mind
A reminder to be kind and grind
To be aligned and intertwined with
A life that redesigns
what was predefined
But yet combined
With the very thread that binds us!